Chinese Health Qigong

Yi Jin Jing

Compiled by the Chinese Health Qigong Association

FOREIGN LANGUAGES PRESS

First Edition 2007
Fourth Printing 2012

ISBN 978-7-119-04778-2

© Foreign Languages Press Co. Ltd, Beijing, China, 2012

Published by
Foreign Languages Press Co. Ltd
24 Baiwanzhuang Road, Beijing 100037, China
http://www. flp. com. cn
E-mail:flp@cipg.org.cn

Distributed by
China International Book Trading Corporation
35 Chegongzhuang Xilu, Beijing 100044, China
P.O. Box 399, Beijing, China

Printed in the People's Republic of China

Contents

Preface

Yi Jin Jing (Tendon-Muscle Strengthening Exercises) is a health and fitness exercise handed down from ancient China. Health Qigong—Yi Jin Jing is part of the New Health Qigong Exercise Series compiled and published by the Chinese Health Qigong Association.

Based on the traditional 12 routines of Yi Jin Jing, Health Qigong—Yi Jin Jing features the same names and key points of the original exercises while putting the theory, skills and effects on the same solid foundation as knowledge of health and fitness Qigong, traditional Chinese medicine and other related scientific fields.

Health Qigong—Yi Jin Jing features extended, soft and even movements displaying a graceful charm, and it puts focus on the turning and flexing of the spine, thus invigorating the limbs and internal organs. These movements have been proved to be able to improve health and fitness, prevent diseases, lengthen life and improve the intellect. In particular, practice of the Yi Jin Jing exercises has very impressive effects on the respiratory system, flexibility, balance and muscular strength. It can also prevent and cure diseases of the joints, digestive system, cardiovascular system and nervous system.

Yi Jin Jing requires the practitioner to keep his or her spirit totally relaxed. It involves an integration of mind and body, natural breathing, gentle movements infused with strength, and an interplay of the insubstantial and the substantial. Easy to learn and perform, this refreshing exercise has impressive health and fitness effects, and is adaptable to all age groups.

Chapter I

Origins and Development

Yi Jin Jing exercises are thought to have their origin in primitive shamanistic rituals. The earliest description of the exercises is found in the *Bibliographic Treatise • History of the Han Dynasty* (汉书•艺文志) almost 2,000 years ago. A brocade painting named *Illustration of Qi Conduction* was unearthed in the 1970s from an ancient tomb in the central China city of Changsha. It has more than 40 illustrations of exercises identifiable as the prototypes of the basic movements of the current Yi Jin Jing exercises.

Yi Jin Jing exercises are widely thought to have been developed by the Indian Buddhist monk Bodhidharma, who was also the originator of the Shaolin martial arts tradition. It is recorded that Bodhidharma arrived at the Shaolin Temple in the Songshan Mountains in central China's Henan Province in 526 AD. According to legend, he was the founder of Zen Buddhism and initiated the Buddhist practice of Dhyana or deep meditation, in China. Monks of the Shaolin Temple played an impressive role in the evolution of the Yi Jin Jing exercises.

As Dhyana featured long and quiet sitting, the monks took up martial arts (Wushu) to limber up their bodies after meditation.

A number of works on Yi Jin Jing appeared during the Song Dynasty (960-1279). Among them was the Cream of Daoist Doctrine compiled by Zhang Junfang by order of the then emperor.

The earliest account of the modern 12-movement exercises is included in the *Illustrations of Internal Exercise* (內功圖说) compiled by Pan Wei in 1858 in the Qing Dynasty.

As traditional Yi Jin Jing relies heavily on the traditional Chinese medicine theory of the Five Elements—metal, wood, water, fire and earth—different schools of the exercises have sprung up emphasizing this aspect in many works.

The Health Qigong—Yi Jin Jing has absorbed the cream of the traditional 12-routine Yi Jin Jing exercises together with a modern scientific approach. The movements form a continuous integrity, focusing on tendon stretching and bone flexing, and combining softness with strength. An essential part of the routines is natural breathing, assisted by calmness of the mind, to make the circulation of the vital energy as unimpeded as possible.

Chapter II
Characteristics

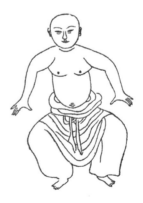

Smooth and Extended Movements to Stretch the Bones and Tendons

Whatever part of the body is being exercised, the Yi Jin Jing movements require a full range of stretching, bending, flexing and twisting in multi-directional and wide-ranging motions of the bones and related joints. As the bones are flexed, the muscle groups and tendons and ligaments are also stretched. This improves the blood circulation and nutrition supersession in the soft tissues of the motion-related areas, increases the flexibility and pliability of such soft tissues as muscles, tendons and ligaments, and enhances the mobility of the bones, joints and muscles.

Soft and Even Movements for Coordinated Grace

The authors have re-compiled the movements of the traditional 12-movement Yi Jin Jing exercises and added links between the various movements, thus making the process clearer and more graceful. The movements of the exercise are multi-directional, the limbs flex in a simple or curved motion and in a natural range of motion with the joints as the axis. The movements are conducted at a slow and even pace. When strength is required, it should be applied in a gradual way, and the muscles should be relaxed to combine strength with tenderness. No complicated or repetitive movements are included, and all the routines feature extended, continuous, graceful, coordinated and quiet movements.

Focus on Spine Turning and Flexing

As the main supporting column of the body, the spine consists of vertebrae, ligaments and the spinal cord.

The Yi Jin Jing exercises are centered on the twisting, flexing and stretching of the spine, with the waist as the axis. Such movements help to stimulate spinal and nerve cords to make them function more effectively, together with the exercise of the limbs and internal organs. The completion of the routines with the integration of a relaxed body and peaceful mind can improve health and fitness, prevent diseases, lengthen life and improve the intellect.

Chapter III

Practice Tips

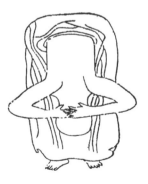

Integration of Mind and Body with a Relaxed Spirit

Yi Jin Jing should be practiced with a relaxed spirit and a peaceful mind. Practitioners do not have to particularly initiate movements by the mind or focus on the intended parts of the body. Rather, the mind follows the movements, and should be coordinated with the circulation of Qi with the body's movements.

Meanwhile, however, concentration is required to accompany individual movements. For example, the mind should concentrate on the palms during the Wei Tuo [Wei Tuo, or Skanda, the temple guardian in Buddhism] Presenting the Pestle 3 routine, and the mind should be focused on the Mingmen point at the back of the waist while fixing the eyes on the upper palm during the routine 4 of Plucking a Star and Exchanging a Star Cluster. The mind should be focused on the palms during the Black Dragon Displaying Its Claws routine. Other movements require imagination, not consciousness, to accompany them. Among them are the Three Plates Falling on the Floor, Displaying Paw-Style Palms like a White Crane Spreading Its Wings, Pulling Nine Cows by Their Tails and Bowing Down in Salutation. These movements should be followed by a relaxed mind, and not hard concentration.

Natural Breathing

Gentle and easy breathing without any gasping or obstruction is required to relax the spirit and body, make the mind peaceful and coordinate the body's motions. Noisy breathing, gasping and distorted nostrils tend to upset the mind, disturb the balance and make the movements uncoordinated.

Free and unrestrained inhalation is particularly required when lifting the hands during the Wei Tuo Presenting the Pestle 3 routine, when expanding the arms and chest during the Pulling Nine Cows by Their Tails routine, and when expanding the arms and chest and relaxing the shoulders during the Nine Ghosts Drawing Swords routine. The reason is that the chest cavity expands and contracts during these movements, and should be allowed to do so freely and to the full.

Free and unrestrained inhalation is particularly required when lifting the hands during the Wei Tuo Presenting the Pestle 3 routine, and when expanding the arms and chest during the Nine Ghosts Drawing Swords routine, while natural exhalation is required when relaxing the shoulders in this routine, when withdrawing the arms in Pulling Nine Cows by Their Tails routine, and when pushing out the palms in Displaying Paw-style Palms like a White Crane Spreading Its Wings routine. The reason is that the chest cavity expands and contracts during these movements, and should be allowed to do so freely and to the full.

Softness in Toughness with the Interplay of the Substantial and Insubstantial

The softness and toughness of the exercise movements interchange throughout the practice. When stretched or relaxed, they display a dialectical relationship of a unity of opposites, in the same way as the reactions of Yin and Yang, the two opposing and interactive aspects of the body according to traditional Chinese medicine. Various movements in the exercise require the practitioners to relax for a while after strength is applied, and suitable force is required after softness or relaxation. In this way, the movements will not be stiff and restrained or slack and fatigued.

While making a distinction between softness and toughness, the exercise aims to achieve a good combination of firmness with gentleness. The movements should be appropriately firm and gentle instead of going to extremes. Otherwise, excessive force could lead to stiff and restrained movements, thus affecting breathing and the mind. On the other hand, excessive softness or relaxation tends to cause slackness, also weakening the intended effect.

Flexibility in Performance and Articulation of "HAI"

The range of movements and extension of postures in Yi Jin Jing are adaptable to people of different ages and physical conditions. For example, practitioners can choose the range of squatting during the Three Plates Falling on the Floor routine. And the exercises should be done step by step from the easier to the more difficult movements.

When squatting and pressing the hands down during the Three Plates Falling on the Floor routine, the sound "HAI" is articulated. This is to assist the passage of the breath and vital energy down to the Dantian point, which is some two inches below the navel. It also has the advantage of avoiding restraint of the lower limbs caused by the squatting motion and upward flow of air back to the head. It also helps to strengthen Dantian and the kidneys. The sound should be produced from the throat, and concentrated at the Yinjiao point on the upper gum (not at the Chengjiang point on the lower gum).

13

Chapter IV

Step-by-Step Descriptions
of the Routines

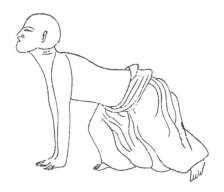

Section 1
Hand and Foot Forms

Basic Hand Forms

| Holding up |

The thumb touches the root of the ring finger, and the other fingers are bent 【Fig. 1】 .

【 Fig. 1 】

Lotus leaf palm

Completely straighten and spread the fingers 【Fig. 2】.

【 Fig. 2 】

Willow leaf palm

Straighten the fingers, and press them together 【Fig. 3】.

【 Fig. 3 】

17

Dragon's paw

Straighten the fingers, and keep them apart, with the thumb, forefinger, ring finger and little finger appropriately withdrawn 【Fig. 4】.

【 Fig. 4 】

Tiger's paw

Keep the fingers apart, with the thumb and forefinger fully apart and the first and second knuckles bent 〖Fig. 5〗.

【 Fig. 5 】

Basic Stances

Bow stance

Keep the legs one big step apart, with a suitable width. Bend the knee of the front leg, keeping it directly above the toes, which should be turned slightly inward. The rear leg should be straight, with the heel and ball of the foot on the floor, and the toes turned slightly inward 〖Fig. 6〗.

【 Fig. 6 】

T-stance

With the feet 10-20 cm apart, bend the knees to adopt a shallow squatting posture. Raise the heel of the front foot, keeping the toes touching the floor close to the middle of the rear foot, and stand firmly on the rear foot 【Fig. 7】.

【 Fig. 7 】

Horse stance

With the feet two to three times their length apart, bend the knees to adopt a half-squatting position, with the thighs slightly raised 【Fig. 8】.

【 Fig. 8 】

Section 2
The Exercises Illustrated

Ready Position

Stand with the feet together and the arms hanging loosely. Pull in the chin slightly, pushing up the head without using force. Close the lips and the teeth. The tongue should touch the upper palate. Look straight ahead 【Fig. 9】.

【 Fig. 9 】

Key points

□ Keep the whole body upright and relaxed. Breathe freely. Look straight ahead without fixing on a specific object. Keep the mind calm.

□ Wrongly positioned hands or feet. Mind in turmoil.

Corrections

□ Adjust the breathing several times to get the body and mind ready for the practice.

Functions and effects

□ It calms the mind, adjusts the breathing, puts the internal organs at ease and straightens the body.

Wei Tuo Presenting the Pestle 1
（韦驮献杵第一式）

Routine 1

1. Move the left foot half a step to the left, so that the feet are about shoulder-width apart. Bend the knees slightly to assume the starting position, with the arms hanging loosely 【Fig. 10】.

【Fig. 10】

2. Raise the arms to shoulder level, with the palms facing each other and the fingers pointing forward 【Figs. 11 and 11A】.

3 and 4. Bend the elbows to withdraw the arms, with the fingers angled at about 30 degrees upward. Hold the palms about 10 cm apart, with the lower ends of the palms located in front of the Danzhong point (at the middle point of an imaginary line linking the nipples). Keep the armpits open. Look straight ahead and down 【Fig. 12】. Pause for a moment.

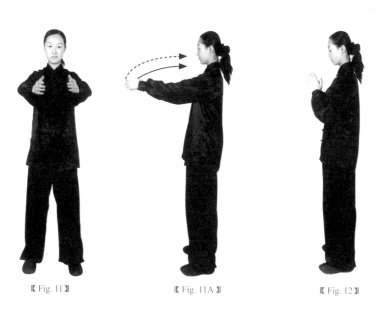

【 Fig. 11 】   【 Fig. 11A 】   【 Fig. 12 】

□ Relax the shoulders and keep the armpits open.

□ Put the palms close to each other in front of the chest, and pause to calm the mind.

Common mistakes

□ Shrugging the shoulders and lifting the elbows or relaxing the shoulders and lowering the elbows when bringing the palms close together in front of the chest.

Corrections

□ Relax, and adjust the movements. Keep the armpits open as if holding an egg in each one.

Functions and effects

□ "When you put your mind in place, the Qi (internal energy) comes back," goes an ancient Chinese saying. When closing the palms and regulate the breath to compose yourself, the mind can be kept at ease and the functions of energy circulation on both sides of the body can be coordinated.

□ This routine also helps to improve the nervous system, regulate the bodily fluids, improve the circulation of the blood, and reduce fatigue.

23

□ Straighten the body, and close palms in front of the chest. Slow your breathing and calm your mind till it is as clear as water. Stand upright in a salutation posture.*

Wei Tuo Presenting the Pestle 2
(韦驮献杵第二式)

Routine 2

1. (Continue from the previous routine) Lift the elbows out from the body and hold the hands at shoulder level in front of the chest, with the fingers pointing to each other and the palms facing down 【Figs. 13 and 13A】.

24

【Fig. 13】   【Fig. 13A】

* From *Twelve Illustrations of Yi Jin Jing* (易筋经十二图) by PanWei, Qing Dynasty; in *Tips of Traditional Chinese Health Care* (中国传统养生珍典), edited by Ding Jihua, et al., the same below.

2. Stretch the arms out, with the palms facing down and the fingers pointing forward 【Figs.14 and 14A】.

【 Fig. 14 】   【 Fig. 14A 】

3. Move the arms to the right and left sides of upper body, respectively, keeping them level with the shoulders, with the palms down and the fingers pointing outward 【Fig. 15】.

【 Fig. 15 】

4. Put the fingers together. Bend the wrists to make the palms upright. Look straight ahead and down 【Fig. 16】 .

【 Fig. 16 】

Key points

□ Apply force at the base of the palms when pushing the palms to the right and left sides.

□ Try to grasp the floor with the toes when bending the wrists and turning the palms upright.

□ Breathe freely and calm the mind.

Common mistake

□ The arms are not lifted to a level position.

Corrections

□ Straighten the arms to a position level with the shoulders when they are lifted.

□ By stretching the upper limbs and pushing the palms out, the channels of the limbs are dredged. This routine also helps to regulate the Qi or internal energy in the heart and lungs, and to improve the breathing and blood and Qi circulation.

□ This routine can help to enhance the muscles of the shoulders and arms, and improve the mobility of the shoulder joints.

□ Keep the arms wide apart when trying to grasp the floor with the toes. Keep your mind at ease and your thoughts calm while looking ahead but concentrating on the Qi within.

Wei Tuo Presenting the Pestle 3
(韦驮献杵第三式)

Routine 3

1. (Continue from the previous routine) Relax the wrists, and move the arms in a curve to the front. Bend the elbows to

put the arms in front of the chest, with the palms down, about the width of a fist from the chest. Look straight ahead and down 【Fig. 17】.

2. Turn the palms outward, and raise them to a position below the ears, with the palms up, thumbs pointing to each other and elbows about level with the shoulders 【Fig. 18】.

【 Fig. 17 】   【 Fig. 18 】

3. Stand on the balls of the feet, with the heels raised. Lift the hands above the head, with the palms up. Spread the shoulders and stretch the elbows. Pull in the chin, with the tongue touching the upper palate. Close the teeth 【Figs. 19 and 19A】.

【 Fig. 19 】   【 Fig. 19A 】

4. Remain motionless in this position for a while.

Key points

□ When lifting the hands, balance your body on the balls of the feet, and apply strength up along the arms and down along the legs. Straighten the spine, and move the body weight slightly forward.

□ The height to which to raise the heels may be adjusted according to the individual conditions of aged practitioners or those in delicate health.

□ Try to transfer the concentration and energy to the hands as they are raised through the Tianmen point (at the top of the head). Look straight ahead and down, and breathe freely.

Common mistakes

□ Elbows are bent when lifting the hands.
□ Raising the head to look upward.

Corrections

□ Straighten the elbows to touch the ears with the arms when lifting and pushing up the hands.

□ Focus the mind on the hands instead of looking at them when they are lifted.

Functions and effects

□ By moving the upper limbs and raising the heels, the Qi or internal energy of Sanjiao, the three portions of the body cavities housing the internal organs, is regulated. Moreover, all the vital energy is mobilized from Sanjiao, from the Sanyin channels of both hands and feet, and from the internal organs.

□ This routine also helps to improve the mobility of the shoulder joints, enhance the strength of the limb muscles, and invigorate the overall blood circulation.

□ Imagine that you are looking up when pushing the hands up above the Tianmen point, and stand on balls of the feet, keeping the upper body straight. Apply strength to the buttocks and to the sides of the upper body. Keep the teeth clenched. Touch the tongue to the upper gums to produce saliva, and regulate the breath through the nose. Feel peace of mind. Withdraw the fists slowly down, and apply strength where needed.

Plucking Stars on Each Side
(摘星换斗势)

Routine 4

31

On the left side:

1. (Continue from the previous routine) Slowly lower the heels. Form fists, with the palm side facing outward, and lower them 【Fig. 20】. Loosen the fingers and make the palms

【Fig. 20】

face downward. Relax the whole body, and look straight ahead and down 【Fig. 21】. Turn the body to the left. Bend the knees, and move the right arm down past the front of the body to outside the left hip bone to "pluck a star," with the right palm open. Move the left arm from the

【 Fig. 21 】

side of the body down to the back of the body, with the back of the hand slightly touching the Mingmen point (at the back of the waist). Look at the right hand【Figs. 22, 23, 24 and 24A】.

【Fig. 22】

【Fig. 23】

【Fig. 24】

【Fig. 24A】

33

2. Straighten the knees and stand upright. Move the right hand past the front of the body upward to the right above the head. Relax the wrist, and bend the elbow slightly with the palm down. The forefingers should point to the left and the middle finger vertical at the Jianyu point (on the shoulder blade). Cover the back of the left hand at Mingmen, with the mind focused on this point. When raising the right hand, following it with the eyes, and keep the eyes fixed on it when it is in position 【Fig. 25】. Remain motionless for a short while, and then move the arms to the sides of the body 【Fig. 26】.

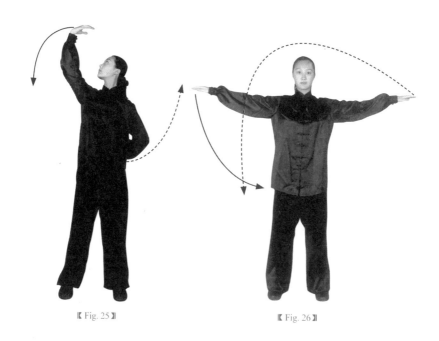

【 Fig. 25 】　　　　　　　【 Fig. 26 】

On the right side:

Repeat the above routine on the right side 【Figs. 27 and 28】.

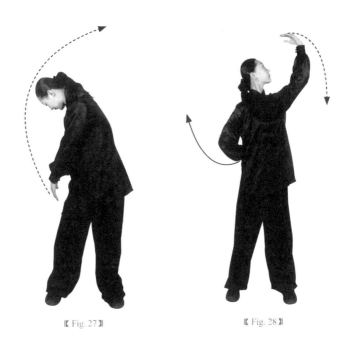

【 Fig. 27 】   【 Fig. 28 】

Key points

□ Move the waist first, and then the shoulders and the arms when turning the body.

□ Focus the mind on Mingmen when looking at the palm. Breath naturally.

□ The range of movements may be adjusted to suit those with neck or shoulder problems.

□ Thrusting out the abdomen when looking up.

□ Inadequate and uncoordinated movements of the arms.

Corrections

□ Relax the waist and pull in the abdomen when looking up.

□ Be relaxed and move waist before moving the arms.

Functions and effects

□ Turning the palms up and down, fixing the eyes on the palms while focusing the mind on Mingmen helps to dispatch the mobilized Qi or the vital energy down to the kidneys and Mingmen. This routine can strengthen the waist and kidneys, and has the effect of preventing aging.

□ It can also enhance the mobility of the neck, shoulders and waist.

Ancient mnemonic rhyme

□ Support the sky with a single hand over the head, and fix the eyes on the palm. Regulate the breath by inhaling through the nose, and apply strength to withdraw your gaze from the left and the right.

Pulling Nine Cows by Their Tails
(倒拽九牛尾势)

Routine 5

1. (Continue from the previous routine) Bend the knees slightly. Move the body weight to the right. Take a step back to the left at about 45 degrees. Turn the right heel inward. Bend the right knee to take a bow stance. Turn the left hand inward. Move it to the front, and then down in a curve to the back of the body. Gradually bend the fingers from the little finger to the thumb to form a fist, and hold it up, with the palm side facing

up. Move the right hand forward and upward in a curve, and gradually bend the fingers from the little finger to the thumb to form a fist, and hold it up a little higher than the shoulder, the palm side facing up. Fix the eyes on the right fist【Fig. 29】.

【Fig. 29】

2. Move the body weight backward. Bend the left knee slightly. Turn the waist slightly to the right before twisting the shoulders and finally the arms. Turn the right arm outward and the left arm inward. Bend the elbows to withdraw the arms. Fix the eyes on the right fist 【Fig. 30】.

【 Fig. 30 】

3. Move the body weight forward. Bend the right knee to form a bow stance. Turn the waist slightly to the left, then the shoulders and finally the arms. Relax the shoulders and stretch the right arm forward and the left arm backward. Fix the eyes on the right fist 【Figs. 31 and 31A】.

【 Fig. 31 】   【 Fig. 31A 】

Repeat the movements 2 and 3 times.

Move the body weight onto the right foot. Withdraw the left foot, and turn the toes of the right foot to the front to assume a starting position with the feet apart. Let the arms hang loose, and look straight ahead and down 【Fig. 32】.

【 Fig. 32 】

Do the above movements from the left side 【Figs. 33, 34, 35 and 35A】.

【 Fig. 33 】

【 Fig. 34 】

【 Fig. 35 】

【 Fig. 35A 】

□ When twisting, start with the waist, followed by the shoulders and finally the arms, with strength applied.

□ Relax the abdomen and fix the eyes on the respective palms.

□ Closely combine stretching forward and backward with the twisting of the waist, applying appropriate force.

□ When taking a back step, be careful to maintain your balance.

Common mistakes

□ Applying excessive force to the arms so that the movements are stiff.

□ Arms are not turned or twisted to the right position.

Corrections

□ Relax the arms to make the movements natural.

□ Make sure that the palm sides of the fists are pushed outward when turning the arms.

41

Functions and effects

□ Turning the waist and shoulder blades can stimulate such points on the back as Jiaji (17 points on each side of the spine), Feishu and Xinshu, dredge the related channels and exercise the heart and lungs.

□ Coordinated motion of the limbs can improve blood

circulation in the soft tissues, and enhance muscle strength and mobility.

□ Move the hips backward and forward, and circulate the Qi in lower abdomen in a relaxed way. Apply force to the arms, and focus your eyes on the relevant fist.

Showing Talons and Spreading Wings
（出爪亮翅势）

Routine 6

42

1. (Continue from the previous routine) Move the body weight onto the left foot. Withdraw the right foot to stand with the feet apart. Turn the right arm outward and the left arm inward, and move them to the sides of the body at shoulder level, with the palms facing forward. Move the arms in a curve to the front of the chest for a hollow hold. Straighten the fingers and putting them together in front of the Yunmen points (below the collarbones), with the palms facing each other and the

fingertips pointing upward. Look straight ahead and down 【Figs. 36, 37, 37A and 38】.

【 Fig. 36 】

【 Fig. 37 】

【 Fig. 37A 】

【 Fig. 38 】

【Fig. 39】

2. Expand the shoulders and chest. Relax the shoulders. Slowly stretch the arms forward, and turn the palms to the front to make lotus leaf palms by completely straightening and separating the fingers. Make the eyes glare【Figs. 39 and 39A】.

44

【Fig. 39A】

3. Loosen the wrists. Bend the elbows, and withdraw the arms to make lotus leaf palms in front of the Yunmen point. Look straight ahead and down 【Figs. 40, 40A and 41】.

【Fig. 40】

【Fig. 40A】

【Fig. 41】

Repeat points 2-3 three to seven times.

□ When moving the hands to the front, keep the body erect, make the eyes glare and apply internal strength through the palms as if to push open a window first and then to topple a mountain. Withdraw the hands like an ebbing tide.

□ Make lotus leaf palms when moving the hands forward, and willow leaf palms when withdrawing them to the front of the Yunmen point.

□ Inhale freely when withdrawing the hands and take a deep breath when moving the hands forward.

Common mistakes

□ The chest is not fully expanded.

□ Application of physical force, not internal strength, when moving the hands forward.

□ Tense breathing.

46

Corrections

□ Pull in the shoulder blades when moving the hands forward.

□ Push out the hands as if pushing open a window or toppling a mountain.

□ Exhale when extending the arms, and inhale when withdrawing them.

Functions and effects

□ The theory of traditional Chinese medicine holds that

"the lungs are the home of the Qi or internal energy, and they regulate the breathing." The movements of the arms, hands, shoulders and chest help to open and close such points as Yunmen and Zhongfu (below Yunmen). They enhance the converging at the chest of fresh air and the body's internal Qi, thus improving both the breathing and the circulation of blood and internal energy.

□ This routine also enhances the strength of the muscles in the chest, back and upper limbs.

| Ancient mnemonic rhyme |

□ Thrust the body, make the eyes glare, and push the hands forcefully forward. Apply strength when withdrawing the hands. Repeat the routine seven times.

Nine Ghosts Drawing Sabers
（九鬼拔马刀势）

Routine 7

1. (Continue from the previous routine) Turn the body to the right. Turn the right hand outward, with the palm up. Turn the

left hand inward, with the palm down 【Figs. 42 and 42A】. Move the right hand from the front of the chest, past the right armpit to the back of the body, with the palm facing out. Move the left hand from the front of the chest to the front, with the palm

【 Fig. 42 】

【 Fig. 42A 】

facing out 【Figs. 43 and 43A】. Turn the body slightly to the left. Lift the right hand past the right side of the body to the front of the head. Bend the elbow. Move the hand in a half circle around the head to cover the left ear. Move the left hand down from beside the left side of the body to the left behind the body. Bend the elbow. Touch the spine with the back of the left hand, with the palm facing back and the fingertips pointing up. Turn the head to the right. Press the left ear with the middle finger of the right hand. Press the Yuzhen point (on the occiput) lightly. Keep

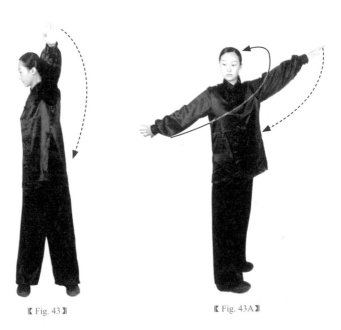

【Fig. 43】　　　　　　　【Fig. 43A】

the gaze fixed on the right hand, and look back to the left when the motion is finished 【Figs. 44, 45 and 45A】.

【 Fig. 44 】

【 Fig. 45 】

【 Fig. 45A 】

2. Turn the body to the right. Expand the arms and chest. Look upward to the right, and maintain this position for a while 【Fig. 46】.

3. Bend the knees. Turn the upper body to the left. Withdraw the right arm. Tuck the chest in. Push the left hand along the spine as far as possible. Look at the right heel, and maintain this position for a while 【Figs. 47 and 47A】.

【 Fig. 46 】

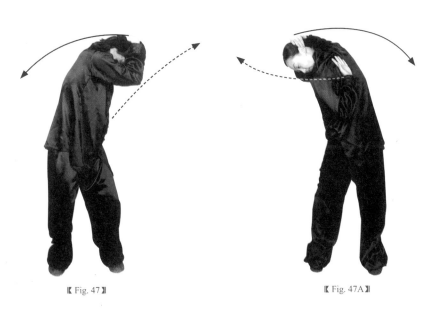

【 Fig. 47 】   【 Fig. 47A 】

Repeat points 2 and 3 three times.

Straighten the knees, and turn the body to face forward. Move the right hand above the head, and down to the right side level to the shoulder. At the same time, lift the left hand from beside the body to shoulder level, both palms down. Look straight ahead and down 【Fig. 48】.

【 Fig. 48 】

From the left side:

Do the above movements from the left side 【Figs. 49, 50 and 51】.

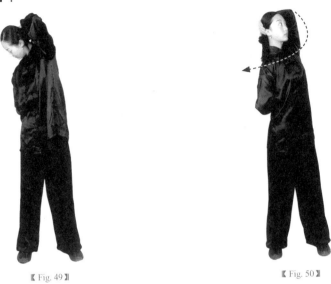

【 Fig. 49 】   【 Fig. 50 】

【 Fig. 51 】

□ Apply as much strength as possible when stretching in different directions. Bend and flex the body in a coordinated and unrestrained way.

□ Breathe naturally when expanding the chest and arms, and exhale normally when relaxing the shoulders and closing the arms.

□ Exhale naturally when closing and lifting the arms, and inhale normally when raising the body and spreading the arms.

□ The turning range of the head can be adjusted, and this routine should be light and slow for the aged and weak and those with hypertension and neck problems.

Common mistakes

□ Relaxing the hand at the back of the body when bending the knees and closing the arms.

□ Moving the body weight to one side when bending the knees to squat.

□ Turning the head too much to the left or right.

Corrections

□ Lift and push up the hand at the back of the body when closing the arms.

□ Keep the body weight stable when raising and lowering the body.

□ Keep relaxed throughout the routine, and avoid turning the head.

□ As the body flexes and stretches, the passages for the Qi or internal energy are opened and closed in a rhythmical way, so that the spleen and stomach are massaged and the kidneys strengthened. The movements also help to dredge such important points as Yuzhen and Jiaji.

□ This routine enhances the strength of the muscles of the neck, shoulders, waist and back, thus improving the mobility of various joints.

□ Turn the head, bend the upper arm, and hold the top of the head and neck. Withdraw the hand from the head, and apply as much strength as possible. Change the position from right to left, while keeping the body erect and breathing naturally.

Sinking the Three Bodily Zones
(三盘落地势)

Routine 8

Move the left foot one step to the left, with the feet shoulder-width apart. The toes should be facing the front. Look straight ahead and down 【Fig. 52】.

1. Bend the knees to adopt a squatting position. At the same time, relax the shoulders and lower the elbows. Lower the hands to a position level with the Huantiao point (on the upper outside of the thigh). Bend the elbows slightly, with the palms facing down and the fingers pointing outward. Look straight ahead and down 【Fig. 53】. Exhale to pronounce the sound "HAI," and place the tongue between the upper and lower teeth at the end of the sound.

【 Fig. 52 】   【 Fig. 53 】

2. Turn the palms upward. Bend the elbows slightly, and lift the arms to the sides level with the shoulders. Slowly stand up. Look straight ahead 【Figs. 54 and 55】.

【 Fig. 54 】

57

【 Fig. 55 】

Repeat points 1 and 2 three times. Squat slightly the first time 【Fig. 56】, take a half squat the second time 【Fig. 57】, and completely squat down the third time 【Fig. 58】.

【Fig. 56】　　　　　　　　　　【Fig. 57】

【Fig. 58】

Key points

□ Relax the waist and tuck in the buttocks when squatting down, as if holding a heavy weight in the hands. When standing up, also imagine to be holding a huge weight.

□ Gradually increase the range of squatting. The range can be adjusted according to individual conditions for the aged and the weak. Young practitioners may assume a half or a compete squat.

□ Keep the upper body straight. Avoid tilting forward or backward, when squatting down and straightening up.

□ When pronouncing the sound "HAI," slightly open the mouth. Apply strength to the Yinjiao point (on the upper jaw). Relax the lower lip. There should be no strength applied to the Chengjiang point (on the lower gum). The sound should be produced from the throat.

□ When making the eyes glare, keep the mouth closed. Place the tongue on the upper palate. Keep the body straight and relaxed.

59

Common mistakes

□ Holding the arms rigid when pressing the palms down and squatting.

□ Forgetting to pronounce the sound "HAI."

Corrections

□ Bend the elbows slightly, and press the palms horizontally down when squatting.

□ Pronounce the sound "HAI" when squatting down.

□ The bending and stretching of the lower limbs combined with the pronunciation of the sound "HAI" help to raise and lower the Qi or internal energy in the chest and abdomen cavities. They also help the exchanges of fluids of the heart and kidneys, and their interaction.

□ In addition, they enhance the strength of the waist, kidneys, abdomen and lower limbs, strengthen the Qi at the Dantian point (about two inches below the navel).

□ Place the tongue on the upper palate and the focus the mind on the teeth while making the eyes glare. Separate the feet when squatting down, and imagine the hands to be holding a heavy weight. When turning the palms up, imagine that they are bearing a heavy weight. Make the eyes glare while the mouth is closed. Stand erect, and with the feet straight.

Black Dragon Displaying Its Claws

（青龙探爪势）

Routine 9

1. (Continue from the previous routine) Withdraw the left foot half a step, with the feet shoulder-width apart (Fig. 59). Form fists, and place the ulnar sides of the fists at the Zhangmen points at the sides of the waist, palm sides facing up. Look straight ahead and down 【Fig. 60】. Loosen the fingers of the right

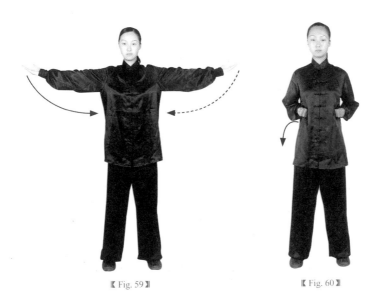

【 Fig. 59 】　　　　　　　【 Fig. 60 】

fist. Straighten the right arm up, and move it down to the outer right side, to a position a bit lower than the shoulders, with the palm up. Fix the gaze on the hand 【Figs. 61 and 62】.

【Fig. 61】

【Fig. 62】

2. Bend the elbow of the right arm, and tuck in the wrist. Make the right palm into a dragon's claw by straightening the fingers and keeping them apart, with the thumb, forefinger, ring finger and little finger appropriately withdrawn, pointing fingertips to the left. Move the hand horizontally leftward, following the movement with the eyes. Turn the body a quarter turn to the left, and look at the direction pointed by the right hand 【Figs. 63, 64 and 64A】.

【 Fig. 63 】

【 Fig. 64 】

【 Fig. 64A 】

3. Loosen the fingers of the right hand. Tilt the upper body to the left and forward, and press the right palm down to the outside of the left foot. Look down 【Figs. 65 and 66】 . Move the left-tilted body to the right and into a forward-tilted position, bringing the right hand in a curve from the front of the left knee to the outside of the

64

【 Fig. 65 】

【 Fig. 66 】

right knee. Turn the right arm outward, the palm facing forward, and make a fist of the right hand. Follow the movement of the hand with the eyes 【Figs. 67 and 68】.

【 Fig. 67 】

【 Fig. 68 】

4. Straighten the body. Withdraw the right fist to the right Zhangmen point, resting both fists at the sides of the waist, with the palm-side up. Look straight ahead and down 【Fig. 69】.

【 Fig. 69 】

From the right side:

Repeat the above routine on the right side 【Figs. 70, 71, 72, 73 and 74】 .

【 Fig. 70 】

【 Fig. 71 】

【 Fig. 72 】

【 Fig. 73 】

【 Fig. 74 】

□ Stretch out the arm to display the Dragon's Claw. When pressing it down in a curve, apply strength to the shoulders and back, with an unrestrained and coordinated motion and complete the movement without a pause.

□ Follow the dragon's claw with the eyes and mind.

□ When pressing down the dragon's claw, the range may be adjusted according to individual conditions of the aged and the weak.

Common mistakes

□ The upper body is tilted forward too much, causing the practitioner to overbalance and bend the knees.

□ Bending the fingers while forming the dragon's claw.

Corrections

68

□ Keep the knees straight when titling the body forward.

□ When straightening the separated fingers, withdraw the thumb, forefinger, ring finger and little finger, with strength applied to the palm.

Functions and effects

□ "The two sides of the waist are in the domain of the liver. The liver is the home of the blood and the kidneys are the home of the reproductive essence," according to the theory of traditional Chinese medicine. Such movements as turning the upper body, displaying the dragon's claw to the left and right, and bending the upper body help to stretch and relax the sides of the chest. They can also dredge the channels of the liver and Qi and smooth the mind and mood, besides improving the mobility of the waist and lower limbs.

□ As the Dragon displays its paws, it starts from the left and finishes at the right. Monks practice making the palms even and putting the mind at ease. Apply strength through the shoulders and back, and lower the hands to below the knees. Look straight ahead to calm the mind and put the thoughts at ease.

Tiger Springing on Its Prey
(卧虎扑食势)

Routine 10

From the left

1. (Continue from the previous routine) Turn the toes of the right foot inward about 45 degrees. Withdraw the left foot to the inside of the right foot to form a T-stance. Turn the body

a quarter of a turn to the left. Place the fists at the Zhangmen points. Look directly forward as the body turns to the left 【Figs. 75 and 75A】.

【 Fig. 75 】

【 Fig. 75A】

〖 Fig. 76 〗

2. Take a big step forward to form a left T-stance. Place the fists at the Yunmen points (near the collarbones). Turn the fists inward to make tiger's paws. Leap forward like a tiger springing at its prey. Bend the elbows slightly. Look straight ahead【Figs. 76 and 76A】.

〖 Fig. 76A 〗

3. Bend and expand the upper body gradually from the waist to the chest, and move the body weight forward. Move the hands in a circle down the body, backward, upward and forward 【Figs. 77, 78 and 79】. Tilt the upper body forward. Press the tiger's paws down to touch the floor with the fingers. Bend the rear

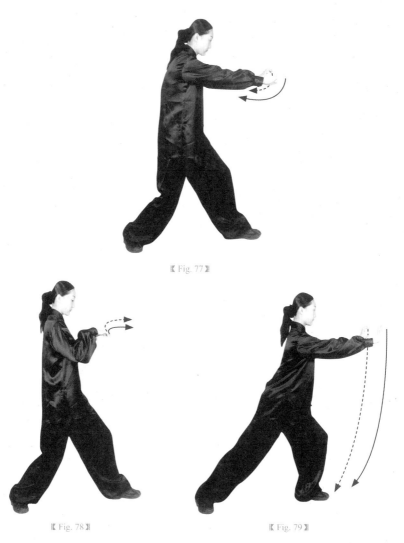

【Fig. 77】

【Fig. 78】

【Fig. 79】

leg to touch the floor with the toes, with the front heel slightly raised. Hold the waist tightly and thrust the chest forward. Raise the head. Make the eyes glare. Maintain this position, look upward straight ahead 【Figs. 80 and 80A】.

【 Fig. 80 】

【 Fig. 80A 】

Aged and weak practitioners may press the tiger's paws only as afar down as the sides of the left knee.

4. Stand up and hold the fists at the Zhangmen points at the sides of the waist. Move the body weight backward. Turn the toes of the left foot about 135° inward, and move the body weight to the left. At the same time, turn the body about 180 degrees to the right. Withdraw the right foot to the inside of the left foot, to form a T-stance 【Fig. 81】.

【 Fig. 81 】

From the left side:

Repeat the above movements on the right side 【Figs. 82 and 83】.

【 Fig. 82 】

【 Fig. 83 】

□ Move the upper body to initiate the springing and circling motions of the hands.

□ Apply strength to the fingertips, and bend the waist backward in a reversed bow when raising the head and making the eyes glare.

□ The range of motion may be adjusted for aged and weak practitioners.

Common mistakes

□ Shrugging the shoulders, tucking in the chest and letting the head sway when tilting the body forward.

□ The fingers are not bent enough or bent too much when making tiger's paws.

Corrections

□ Stand erect, and look straight ahead and up.

□ Apply strength to the tips of the fingers when they are bent.

Functions and effects

□ The theory of the traditional Chinese medicine holds that the Renmai meridian or conception vessel is the source of the Yin meridians, and directs the Yin meridians all over the body. The tilting backward of the body and the flexing of the chest and abdominal cavities help to dredge the Renmai meridian and regulate the Qi or internal energy flowing through the Sanyin meridians of the hands and feet.

□ This routine also improves the mobility of the muscles of the waist and legs.

| Ancient mnemonic rhyme |

□ When squatting with the weight resting on both feet, tilt the body and flex the left and right buttocks alternately. Raise the head, and thrust the chest out. Tilt the waist forward until it is as level as a grindstone. Breathe steadily and evenly through the nose, touching the fingers to the floor for support. Although it takes supernatural figures to subdue dragons and tigers, it'll enhance your health if you learn such skills.

Bowing Down in Salutation
(打躬势)

Routine 11

1. (Continue from the previous routine) Raise the upper body, move the body weight backward, and turn to face forward. Turn the toes of the right foot inward, with the toes pointing

forward. Withdraw the left foot, to stand with the feet apart. When turning the body to the left, loosen the hands, and turn them outward, with the palms facing forward. Raise them to the sides at shoulder level. Bend the elbows to cover the ears with the palms, and press the nape of the neck with the fingers, with the fingers pointing to each other. Tap this area seven times with the index and middle fingers. Look straight ahead and down 【Figs. 84 and 85】 .

【 Fig. 84 】   【 Fig. 85 】

2. Tilt the upper body forward, and slowly stretch and flex from the cervical, thoracic and lumbar vertebrae down to the coccygeal vertebrae. Straighten the thighs, fix the eyes on the toes, and remain in this position for a while 【Figs. 86 and 86A】.

【 Fig. 86 】

【 Fig. 86A 】

3. Gradually straighten the upper body, starting with the coccygeal vertebrae, through the lumbar, thoracic and cervical vertebrae up to the head. Cover the ears with the palms, and press the nape of the neck with the fingers pointing to each other. Look straight ahead and down 【Fig. 87】.

【 Fig. 87 】

Repeat points 2 and 3 three times; gradually increase the motion range when tilting and bending the upper body forward, pausing for a while. Bend the upper body forward less than 90 degrees the first time, about 90 degrees the second time, and more than 90 degrees the third time 【Figs. 88, 88A, 89, 89A, 90 and 90A】 .

【 Fig. 88 】

【 Fig. 88A 】

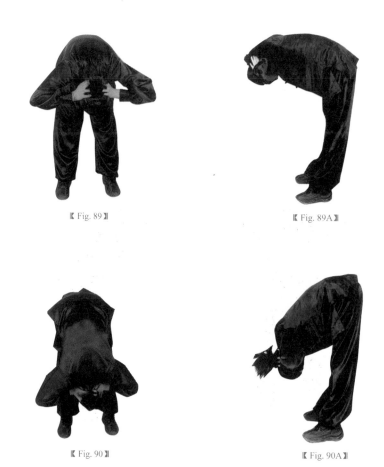

【 Fig. 89 】　　　　　　　　【 Fig. 89A 】

80

【 Fig. 90 】　　　　　　　　【 Fig. 90A 】

Aged and weak practitioners may restrict the bend to about 30, 45, and 90 degrees, respectively.

□ Keep knees straight, and turn the elbows outward when bending the upper body.

□ When tilting the upper body forward, try to stretch and flex the spine so that the neck and head are bent like a hook; when tilting the body backward, gradually stretch the spine from the coccygeal vertebrae up.

□ The range of tilt should be adjusted according to the individual conditions of aged and weak practitioners.

Common mistakes

□ Bending the knees and moving too quickly when bending and raising the upper body.

Corrections

□ Relax the body and mind when bending and raising the upper body, and keep the legs straight.

81

Functions and effects

□ The theory of traditional Chinese medicine holds that the Dumai meridian (governor vessel) is one of the Yang meridians, and governs the Qi or the vital energy flowing through the Yang meridians, including those passing through the cervical, thoracic and lumbar vertebrae down to the coccygeal vertebrae. If it is fully exercised, all the Qi or the vital energy in those channels will be mobilized and transferred throughout the body to enhance overall health and fitness.

□ This routine can also improve the mobility of the waist, back and lower limbs, to enhance the functions of the waist and legs.

□ Tapping the nape of the neck helps to refresh the brain, increase the hearing capacity and reduce brain fatigue.

| Ancient mnemonic rhyme |

□ With both hands holding the head, bend the upper body down to about the level of the knees. Lower the head, and clench the teeth. Rest the tongue on the upper palate, and apply strength to the elbows. Cover the ears to improve the hearing, and regulate the energy circulation to calm the mind.

Swinging the Tail
（掉尾势）

Routine 12

(Continue from the previous routine) Stand erect, and lift the hands off the ears with a deft movement 〔Fig. 91〕 Stretch the arms forward with the

〖 Fig. 91 〗

fingers interlaced and palms facing oneself 【Figs. 92 and 93】 .
Bend the elbows, and push the hands out, with the palms facing
outward (Figs. 94 and 94A). Bend the elbows, turn the palms down,

【 Fig. 92 】

【 Fig. 93 】

【 Fig. 94 】

【 Fig. 94A 】

and withdraw them to the front of the chest. Tilt the upper body forward, tighten the waist and raise the head. Press the hands down slowly, with fingers interlaced. Look straight ahead【Figs. 95, 96 and 96A】.

【 Fig. 95 】

【 Fig. 96 】

【 Fig. 96A】

Aged and weak practitioners may bend the upper body forward, with the head raised, and slowly press the hands down to in front of the knees.

1. Turn the head left to look back. Meanwhile, move the buttocks forward to the left, and look back at where the sacrum is located 【Figs. 97 and 97A】 .

【 Fig. 97 】

【 Fig. 97A 】

2. Keep the fingers interlaced, then relax the palms and raise the head to face forward 【Fig. 98】 .

【 Fig. 98 】

3. Turn the head right to the back. Meanwhile, move the buttocks forward to the right. Look back at where the sacrum is located (Figs. 99).

4. Keep the fingers interlaced, then relax the palms and raise the head to face forward 【Fig. 100】.

【 Fig. 99 】

【 Fig. 100 】

Repeat points 1-4 three times.

Key points

□ Turn the head and move the buttocks in such a way that the head and buttocks move toward each other.

□ The motion of the head should be slow, and the range of turning should be reduced for aged and weak practitioners, and those with hypertension or neck problems. The bending of the body and the moving of the buttocks may be adjusted to suit the individual conditions of the practitioners.

□ Coordinate the movements with natural breathing, and the

mind should be concentrated on the movements.

Common mistakes

- □ Moving the head and arms in the wrong way.
- □ Moving the hands and body weight to the left or right.

Corrections

□ Keep the interlaced hands steady after pressing them down, and try to feel the coordination between the shoulder and the hipbone on the same side.

Functions and effects

□ Bending the body, raising the head and swinging the buttocks to the left and right can integrate the vital energy especially in the Dumai and Renmai meridians, as well as in all the other channels of the body. This routine loosens the whole body for total relaxation.

□ It can also enhance the strength of the waist and back muscles and improve the mobility of the various joints and muscles along the spine.

87

Ancient mnemonic rhyme

□ Straighten the knees, spread the arms and push the hands down to the floor. Raise the head, make the eyes glare, and the mind focused.

Closing Form
(收势)

1. (Continue from the previous routine) Loosen the fingers, spread the arms outward, and stand straight. Meanwhile lift the straightened arms to the sides at shoulder level, with the palms up. Raise the arms over the head, with the elbows bent and the palms down. Look straight ahead and down 【Figs. 101, 102 and 103】 .

【 Fig. 101 】

【 Fig. 102 】

【 Fig. 103 】

2. Relax the shoulders. Bend the elbows, and withdraw the hands past the head, face and chest to the front of the abdomen, with the palms down. Look straight ahead and down 【Fig. 104】.

Repeat points 1 and 2 three times.

【 Fig. 104 】

Relax the arms, and let them hang down by the sides of the body. Withdraw the left foot, and stand straight, with the feet together. Rest the tongue on the upper palate. Look straight ahead 【Fig. 105】.

【 Fig. 105 】

89

□ When the hands are moved down the first two times, concentrate the mind on the motion down to the floor, through the Yongquan points on the soles of the feet. When the hands are moved down for the third time, the mind should follow the motion down to the abdomen, and linger there.

□ When moving the hands downward, the motion should be slow and even-paced.

Common mistakes

□ Raising the head to look up when lifting the arms.

Corrections

□ Keep the head straight up, and look straight ahead and down.

Functions and effects

□ Lifting the hands can guide the Qi or internal energy back to the Dantian point (some two inches below the navel).

□ It can also help to relax all the muscles and joints in the body.

Acupuncture Points
Mentioned in This Book

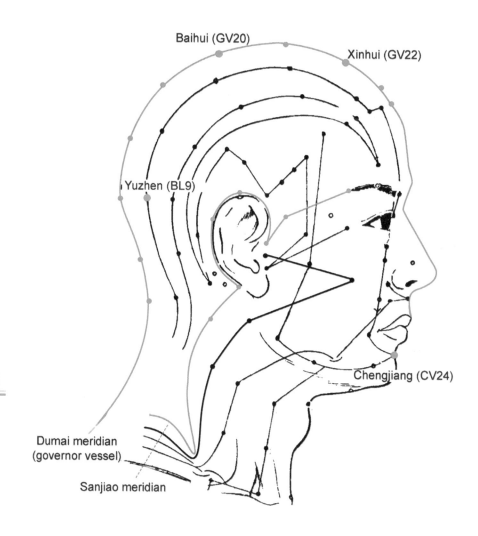

Baihui (GV20)

Xinhui (GV22)

Yuzhen (BL9)

Chengjiang (CV24)

Dumai meridian
(governor vessel)

Sanjiao meridian

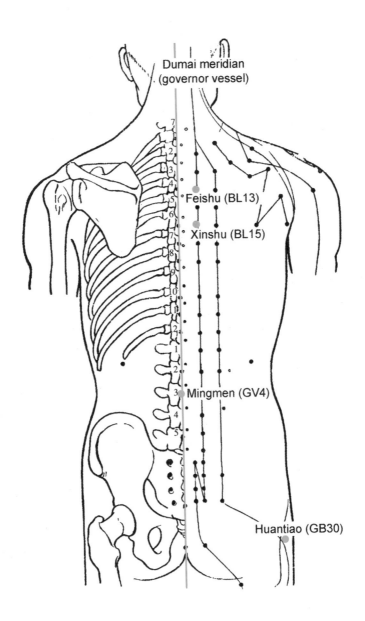

Dumai meridian
(governor vessel)

Feishu (BL13)

Xinshu (BL15)

Mingmen (GV4)

Huantiao (GB30)

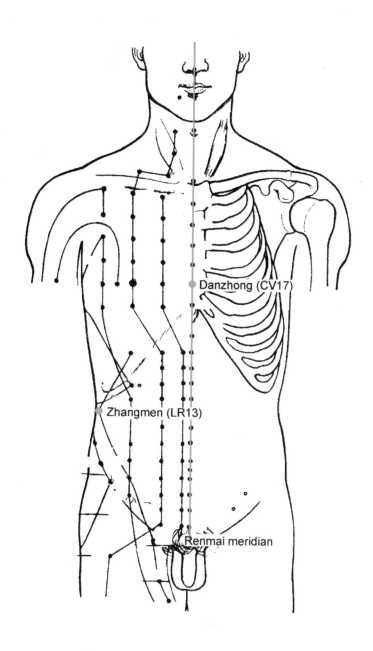

Danzhong (CV17)

Zhangmen (LR13)

Renmai meridian

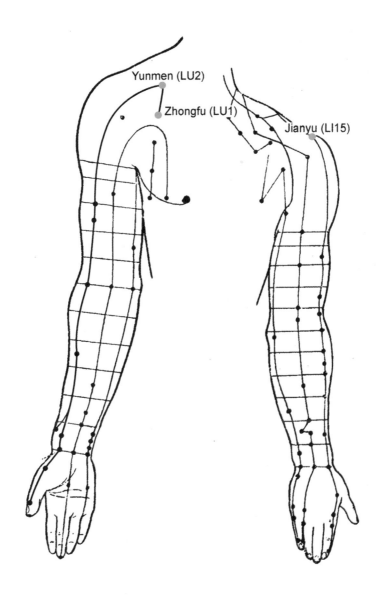

Yunmen (LU2)

Zhongfu (LU1)

Jianyu (LI15)

图书在版编目（CIP）数据

易筋经：英文/国家体育总局健身气功管理中心编.
北京: 外文出版社, 2012年
　(健身气功丛书)
　ISBN 978-7-119-04778-2
　I.易...　II.国...　III.易筋经（古代体育）–英文 IV. G852.6
中国版本图书馆CIP数据核字（2007）第045690号

英文翻译：周宗欣
英文审定：Parul White　郁苓
责任编辑：杨春燕　杨璐
印刷监制：张国祥

健身气功——易筋经

国家体育总局健身气功管理中心　编

©2012 外文出版社有限责任公司

出版发行：

外文出版社有限责任公司（中国北京百万庄大街24号　100037）

http://www.flp.com.cn

电　　话：008610－68320579（总编室）
　　　　　008610－68995852（发行部）
　　　　　008610－68327750（版权部）

制　　版：北京维诺传媒文化有限公司
印　　刷：北京外文印刷厂
开　　本：787mm×1092mm　1/16
印　　张：6.5
2012年8月第1版第4次印刷
（英文）
ISBN 978-7-119-04778-2
07000（平装）

14-E-3785P